GW01255284

Sports

Mary O'Keeffe

g GILL EDUCATION

Do you
like sports?
There are lots
of sports to
pick from,
so you should
like one!

We like lots of sports in school.

We do them in the school hall.
We do sports on the yard too.
Let's have a look at what
sports we do in school!

We do a lot of running. We run fast and we jog too.

It is good to try your best, but you do not have to be first!

What sports do you do?

I like sports, because they are good for me. Here we are. We like to skip.

When you start a sport, you will have to get some bits of kit.

You can go to the **sports shop**.

Tell them what sport you want to do.

They will help you find what you need.

They will give you some tips!

They are there to help you.

The gloves will help his grip.

Are you on a **team**?
Some sports, like soccer and
hurling, are **team** sports.
It's good to be on a **team**,
because you can have lots of
pals on your **team**.
You work as a **team** too.

Sports by yourself
are lots of fun too.
You can get really
good at them.
You have to push
yourself and do your
best when you can!

It is good fun to look at sports too. You can yell for the best **team**! You can see sports on the TV or you can go and see them in your town.

It's nice to spend time with your family.

You can go with Mam and Dad to see some sports. What sports do they like?

In school,
we have
Sports Day.

Do you?

I like the fact that I get
to do sports all day long!
Teacher has a big list of
sports for us to do!

It is a long day, but we have a lot of fun

We get to go on the grass!

We get medals at the end of Sports Day.

Sports are good for you and for me.
You can get fit and have fun.
Sports are good for your mind too!